A Beekeeper's Year

by **Sylvia A. Johnson**
Photographs by **Nick Von Ohlen**

Little, Brown and Company

BOSTON   NEW YORK   TORONTO   LONDON

Acknowledgments

For their participation in the making of this book, the author and
photographer wish to thank honey house helpers Kristina and Nathan Knutson,
John Nelson, Jay Reipke, Breanna and Lynsey Wetzler, and especially
beekeeper John Wetzler and his wife and co-worker, Mary Ann.

Thanks also to manuscript consultant Dr. Marla Spivak, Assistant Professor and Beekeeper,
Department of Entomology, University of Minnesota.

Additional photographs courtesy of Orley R. Taylor, Jr. (page 16)
and Elizabeth M. Petersen (title page, pages 12 and 25)

First Edition

Library of Congress Cataloging-in-Publication Data
Johnson, Sylvia A.
    A beekeeper's year / by Sylvia A. Johnson ; photographs by Nick
Von Ohlen. — 1st ed.
        p.   cm.
    Summary: Follows a beekeeper through the four seasons, showing how
bees and humans work together to make honey.
    ISBN 0-316-46745-6
    1. Bee culture — Juvenile literature.   2. Honeybee — Juvenile
literature.   [1. Bee culture. 2. Honeybee.]   I. Von Ohlen, Nick,
ill.   II. Title.
SF523.5.J64   1994
638'.1—dc20   93-10199

                        10 9 8 7 6 5 4 3 2 1
                                    sc
                    Published simultaneously in Canada
                    by Little, Brown & Company (Canada) Limited

                        Printed in Hong Kong

A Beekeeper and His Bees

What do you do when you hear the buzz of a bee? Do you wave your arms, or scream and run? This is what many people do, but not John Wetzler. John is a beekeeper, and he likes to hear that buzzing sound. It tells him that his bees are hard at work.

John and his wife, Mary Ann, make their home in Minnesota, a state that is one of the nation's leading producers of honey. The Wetzlers live in southwestern Minnesota, in a small house on the banks of the Des Moines River. In the yard next to the house are stacks of white boxes, some more than six feet high. These are bee hives. John has twenty-four hives in all, ten at his place and the rest on a farm nearby.

John and Mary Ann don't make a living keeping bees. John is a retired high school teacher. For the Wetzlers, as for many other people in rural areas, beekeeping is a hobby. About two hundred thousand American beekeepers are *hobbyists,* who own fewer than twenty-five hives.

A beehive is made up of wooden boxes called hive bodies.

Like many hobbyists, John Wetzler is a beekeeper for only one reason: he likes working with bees. "Keeping bees is different from owning cows or chickens," he says. "That's because honeybees are not really domesticated animals." Bees in a hive behave in just the same way as bees in the wild. Like wild bees, they collect flower *nectar* to make honey for food. And they make as much honey as they possibly can. "There's no such thing as too much honey for a colony of bees!" says John. Since the beekeeper also wants a lot of honey, his main job is to assist his bees in doing what comes naturally.

The relationship between humans and honeybees goes back thousands of years. In prehistoric times, people took honey from the hives of wild bees in hollow trees. About four thousand years ago, the Egyptians kept bees in cigar-shaped hives made of clay. During the Middle Ages, beekeepers used dome-shaped hives called skeps, which were woven of straw.

John Wetzler, like most modern beekeepers, uses hives made of wood. A hive consists of several boxes, or *hive bodies*, which are open at the top and bottom. Hanging inside each hive body are ten movable wooden *frames*. The frames hold sheets of wax called *foundation*, on which bees build the six-sided cells of their combs.

The inner cover of a hive

Wooden frames inside a hive

A frame holds a sheet of foundation on which bees build their wax cells.

The *colony* of bees that lives in one of John Wetzler's hives is just like a colony in the wild. It is made up of thousands of bees, as many as sixty thousand in a large colony. Most are *worker bees* (all females), which do different jobs around the hive. There is one *queen bee*. She is the mother of the colony and the only one that lays eggs. Each colony also has a small number of male bees, called *drones*, which serve as mates for queens.

Whether a colony of bees lives in a wooden hive or in a hollow tree, its activities are determined by the seasons. The cold winter is a quiet time for bees. But with the first breath of spring, the hive starts buzzing and the beekeeper's year begins.

A Beekeeper's Tools

In Minnesota, a beekeeper's outdoor work doesn't really get started until April. By then, most of the snow has melted, and the air is filled with the rich smell of wet earth. Maple trees have burst into bloom, their tiny flowers clustered high on the branches. On a bright morning in early April, John Wetzler finishes his bowl of oatmeal sweetened with honey and gets ready to check his hives.

First John puts on his bee suit, a kind of coverall that fastens tight at the wrists and ankles. He also gets out his hat with its heavy veil. The zipper at the bottom of the veil connects with a zipper around the neck of the suit. This outfit is designed to keep out angry bees that might sting someone disturbing their hive.

Despite this protection, beekeepers do get stung. Most eventually develop a kind of immunity to bee venom, so that stings don't really bother them. John Wetzler says he is glad that bees sting. "If they didn't, a lot more people would probably take up beekeeping."

After he is dressed, John collects his beekeeping tools. His most important piece of equipment is his *smoker*. A smoker does just what its name suggests: it produces smoke from material burned inside it. John burns old twine, which smolders a long time and makes plenty of thick, cool smoke.

When John opens a hive, he puffs smoke on the bees, using the bellows attached to the smoker. Smoke makes bees react as if their hive is on fire. Preparing for escape, they hurry to the honey stores and load up on honey. A bee carrying honey isn't able to sting very well. Smoking bees makes it safer and easier for the beekeeper to do his work.

The other piece of equipment that John takes to the bee yard is his *hive tool*. This small metal tool is used to open hives and loosen frames. Bees seal up cracks in their hive with a sticky substance called *bee glue*. The beekeeper has to break these seals to look inside.

Before he can open his hives this April morning, John must first remove the black plastic wrapping that has protected them during the long winter. With that job done, he carefully takes the cover off each hive and puffs smoke inside. Then he peers in to see what the bees are doing.

A beekeeper's equipment includes a veiled hat, a hive tool, and a smoker.

Blowing smoke on bees makes them easier to handle.

7

Looking for Brood

As part of his spring check, John removes a few frames from each hive to look for *brood:* eggs and developing young bees. Queen bees usually start laying eggs in February. By April, the hive should be brimming with new life. The first hive John opens today has plenty of brood. But when he takes a frame from the second hive, he sees a lot of empty cells. Something has definitely gone wrong here.

Maybe the bees have run out of food. Hungry bees need to be fed with sugar syrup, a mixture of water and granulated sugar. John gives them syrup in a bucket with small holes in the lid. He turns the bucket upside down on top of the opening in the hive's inner cover. The bees come to the opening to get the syrup oozing from the bucket.

If a hive has a shortage of brood, the problem may be a queen who is not laying enough eggs. This hive will need a new queen, and quickly too. If young bees are not produced in spring, then the colony will not have enough workers in the busy summer season. John has ordered some new queens from a bee supplier in Georgia. When they arrive, he will install them in the hives.

A frame of brood

After checking each hive, John makes a record of its condition. "It's not easy writing notes while wearing heavy gloves," John explains, "so I've developed my own record-keeping system." He puts a brick on top of each hive. The position of the brick tells him at a glance what the condition of the hive is.

John's Brick Code

Brick Lengthwise
    flat: everything OK
    edge: inspection needed
Brick Across
    flat: hive being fed
    edge: needs feeding
Brick Diagonal
    flat: colony requeened
    edge: colony needs queen

A "Queenright" Hive

Yesterday John got a call from the post office in town. The clerk told him that he had received a package from Georgia. It was making a buzzing sound. Could he please come in and pick it up? Right away?

The package contained twelve queen bees, each one in a small wooden cage with a screen in the top. Also in each cage were some worker bees, which fed and took care of the queen while she was traveling. Today John is going to put the new queens in the hives.

Opening the first hive, John searches for the old queen. You might think it would be hard to find her among the thousands of bees in the colony. But the queen bee is not hard to spot. She is almost twice as large as the worker bees. The queen also stands out because she is usually surrounded by her "court," a group of worker bees who are feeding and grooming her.

John takes each frame out of the hive and quickly runs his eyes over it. When he finds the queen, he removes her. Now the hive is ready for a new queen, but John can't just drop her in. The worker bees don't know her, and they won't be ready to accept her. They might even kill her. So John puts the queen in the hive while she is still inside her cage. He takes out the attendant bees and pushes the cage down between two frames in the middle of the hive.

A new queen is shipped in a cage.

At one end of the queen cage is a candy plug.

When John puts the cage in the hive, the bees will chew through the plug to release the queen.

10

The queen cage has a hole at one end with a piece of soft sugar candy stuck in it. When the bees in the hive discover the cage, they start to chew through the candy plug. It will take them about three days to eat all the candy. This should give them enough time to get acquainted with the new queen. Through the screen of her cage, they will learn her special smell.

By the time the queen crawls out of the cage, the bees should be ready to accept her and work for her. The hive will have a healthy young queen. In the language of beekeepers, it will be *queenright*.

A queen bee surrounded by her "court"

When dandelions and fruit trees bloom, both the beekeeper and the bees are busy.

Other Spring Jobs

In addition to requeening hives, John Wetzler has other spring work to do in the bee yard. He gives his bees medication to make sure they don't get diseases caused by bacteria. He also sets up some new hives with package bees, bees ordered from a supplier. Each package contains a caged queen and enough workers to start a colony.

Another spring job is uniting hives that are too weak to survive on their own. To combine two hives, John first removes one of the queens. Then he places a sheet of newspaper over one hive and puts the other hive on top of it.

Bees don't like paper in their living area, and they hurry to chew it up. Just like the candy in the queen cage, the newspaper gives bees that don't know each other the chance to get acquainted. By the time the paper is gone, the bees from both hives will be ready to live and work together. Instead of two weak hives, there will be one strong hive.

Feeding bees antibiotics mixed with sugar keeps them healthy.

John shakes the package bees into the new hive.

Bees at Work

While the beekeeper is busy with his spring chores, the bees are hard at work too. Each day, more young bees emerge from their cells and join the hive work force.

During the first twenty days of their lives, workers do indoor jobs. As "house bees," they clean and repair cells and feed developing young bees. They may spend some time as guards, protecting the hive from intruders such as wasps. House bees also receive nectar and *pollen* from *foragers* returning to the hive. As the nectar is passed along, enzymes in the bees' bodies start the process that turns it into honey.

When a worker is about twenty days old, she is ready to become a forager, or field bee. To prepare for this job, she makes short flights around the hive. After the bee has learned to recognize the hive and find her way home, she starts on her foraging trips.

On a warm summer day, a forager may make as many as ten trips. During each one, she collects nectar or pollen from around one hundred flowers. Despite this hard work, a forager produces only one-twelfth of a teaspoon of honey during the six short weeks that she lives!

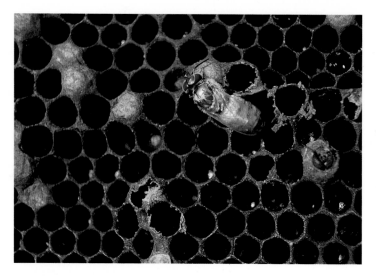

This young worker bee has just hatched.

A worker sucks up syrup with her long tongue.

The Nectar Flow

When a bee goes out to forage for nectar, she usually looks for flowers growing within half a mile of her hive. Beekeepers make sure to locate their hives in areas where there are plenty of flowering plants. What kinds of flowers do bees get nectar from? That depends on the location and the season.

In southwestern Minnesota, where John Wetzler lives, the first major *nectar flow* starts when dandelions bloom in April and May. Beekeepers don't hate dandelions the way most people do, because the yellow flowers are an important source of nectar and pollen. The honey made from dandelion nectar is strong and bitter. John leaves it in the hives for the bees to eat. It tastes just fine to them and provides the energy they need to do their work.

As the days become longer in June, other flowers appear. In the fields near John Wetzler's place, sweet clover and alfalfa begin to bloom. These crops, which are used as feed for livestock, have small, inconspicuous flowers. But they provide the main source of honey for John and most beekeepers in the Midwest.

In other parts of the country, honey comes from crops such as oranges and buckwheat or from wildflowers. Different flower nectars produce honeys with different colors and flavors. Clover honey and orange-blossom honey are light colored and mild in taste, while buckwheat honey is dark and strong.

After leaving the hive, a swarm clusters on a tree branch. Soon the bees will move on to their new home.

Preventing Swarms

When the clover and alfalfa bloom, John Wetzler's bees have plenty of nectar for eating and for making honey. The colonies grow rapidly, reaching their highest numbers. John is glad that his hives are thriving, but now he has something else to worry about. Are his bees going to *swarm*?

When a colony swarms, about half of the bees in a hive fly away, taking the old queen with them. They find a new place to live, usually in a hollow tree or rock crevice. Back in the bee yard, the hive they left behind will have a new young queen and many fewer workers. It will not produce much honey this season.

"When things get too crowded in a hive, you're likely to have swarms," John says. If most of the cells are full and the bees can't move around freely, they may decide to look for more roomy accommodations.

As crowding becomes worse in a hive, *queen cells* begin to appear along the bottoms of the frames. A hive that is preparing to swarm needs a new queen to take the place of the old one, who will leave with the swarm.

So workers start building queen cells, the special large cells where queen bees are raised. The young bees that hatch out of eggs laid in these cells will be fed a steady diet of *royal jelly*. This rich food produced by the worker bees' bodies turns an ordinary female bee into a queen.

When John Wetzler looks in a hive and sees a lot of queen cells, he knows that he has to act fast. He removes the cells, scraping them off with his hive tool. But the bees will just keep making queen cells. What they really need is more room. John may put on another hive body filled with frames that already have wax cells on them. He might also divide the crowded hive and make it into two smaller hives.

These steps can often prevent a hive from swarming, but sometimes they don't work. "Some hives are just determined to swarm," John explains, "and there's nothing the beekeeper can do to stop them."

When a hive becomes too crowded, worker bees build queen cells. Removing the cells may help to prevent swarming.

17

Supering Up

In southwestern Minnesota, the early part of July, with its long sunny days, is the peak of the honey season. The beekeeper's main job at this time of year is to give the bees someplace to store all the honey they are producing. He does this by putting *super*s on his hives.

Supers are small boxes containing frames and wax combs. They are stacked on top of the hive bodies, where the bees live and raise their young. When the bees find these extra storage places, they begin putting honey in them. As long as the nectar flow lasts, the bees will fill super after super. How many supers does John put on a hive? "Usually four or five, but I've had as many as nine," the beekeeper says with quiet satisfaction. When the supers start piling up, John has to use a stepladder to reach the ones on top.

John wants to have only honey in his supers. But if the queen gets into this part of the hive, she will lay eggs there. To prevent this, John uses a *queen excluder*. He places this sheet of plastic between the upper hive body and the first honey super. The openings in the excluder are too small for the large queen to pass through. But they are just the right size for the worker bees. The workers can store honey in the cells of the supers, while the queen is busy down below laying eggs in the hive bodies.

John puts a super on a hive.

Adding a queen excluder

18

Taking Honey

In Minnesota, summer begins winding down in August. The weather is still hot, and corn plants are heavy with ears of yellow corn. But many of the summer flowers are gone. In fields and road ditches, tall spikes of goldenrod begin to appear. At night, the loud, shrill chorus of insects sends a message that autumn is just around the corner.

In the bee yard, the supers are full of mild, light-colored honey made from a combination of clover and alfalfa nectars. It is time for the beekeeper to start taking his share. John Wetzler removes a frame of honey when at least three-quarters of the cells have wax caps on them. Bees makes these caps to protect the honey from moisture. Beekeepers know that capped honey is ripe and ready to extract.

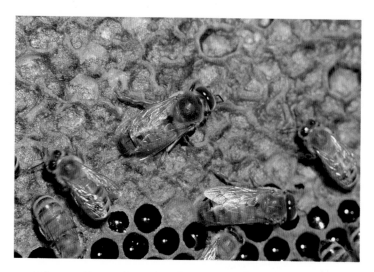

A frame of honey is ready to be removed when most of its cells are capped.

To take honey from a hive, John uses a bee repellant.

When you remove frames from a hive, you also remove the bees clinging to them. John doesn't want bees buzzing around inside his honey house. If he is taking only a few frames, he brushes the bees off. To remove a whole super, he uses a bee repellant.

A repellant is a bad-smelling chemical that bees hate. The one John uses is called Bee Go. He sprinkles it on the cloth pad of a *fume board*. Then he puts the board, pad side down, on top of the super he wants to take. The repellant drives most of the bees down into the lower part of the hive. Then the beekeeper can remove the super and brush away the remaining bees.

John has to be careful to cover up the honey-filled supers as soon as he removes them. If he doesn't, bees from surrounding hives will be attracted by the sweet smell. They may come zooming in to open the cells and steal the honey. Once bees become robbers, they will invade other bees' hives to take honey.

Before starting work in the honey house, John shows his young helpers some bees in a glass-walled observation booth.

In the Honey House

John Wetzler's honey house is a small building not far from the bee yard. It has large glass windows and a concrete floor that is usually a little sticky. Along the walls are stacks of supers. The air is warm and heavy with the sweet smell of honey.

In the honey house, honey is taken from the frames and put into glass jars. The extracting process is simple, but it has several steps. John often has people helping him with it. Today his wife, Mary Ann, and some neighborhood children are lending a hand.

21

The first step in the extracting process is cutting the wax caps off the honey-filled cells. John uses a large knife that is heated electrically. Propping a frame up over the *decapping tank*, he carefully slices off the caps, first on one side and then on the other. The wax caps fall down into the tank, along with some trickles of honey. But most of the honey stays in the cells because the clever bees have built them to slant upward.

Once a frame is uncapped, John and his helpers place it in the *honey extractor*. This barrel-shaped machine has a rack that holds twelve frames. When the extractor is full, John turns on the motor and the machine spins like a washing-machine tub. The rapid spinning pulls the honey from the cells and throws it against the walls of the extractor. It runs down and collects at the bottom, where it is drawn out through a spigot.

An electric knife makes decapping easy.

The decapped frames go into the extractor. After the honey is extracted from the cells, it is drained into buckets.

23

Bottled and labeled, the honey is ready for market.

While John uncaps more frames, his helpers drain the honey from the extractor and put it into buckets. Filters over the tops of the buckets catch bits of wax and other impurities. The bucketfuls of honey are then poured into bottling pails. Mary Ann is in charge of the bottling. Turning the spigot on and off, on and off, she and her assistants fill jar after jar with pale golden honey.

Putting labels on the jars is the final step. Now the honey is ready to be loaded into boxes and taken to farmers' markets in nearby towns. John and Mary Ann spend many sunny late-summer afternoons at the markets, selling honey and answering questions about beekeeping. Sometimes Mary Ann tells people about the delicious cookies, muffins, and breads that can be made using honey. "Let's get an extra jar so we can make some!" says a young customer.

Shoppers at the farmers' market can buy fresh flowers, golden honey, homegrown fruits and vegetables, and sweet-smelling candles made from beeswax.

Chores in Autumn

When the leaves of the oak trees around John Wetzler's place turn gold and clumps of purple asters dot the fields, it is time for autumn chores in the bee yard.

During September, the bees continue to gather the last nectar of the year from late-blooming flowers such as goldenrod and asters. After the first frost, usually in late September, the flowers are gone, and the honey season is over.

On a crisp day in early October, John goes from hive to hive, gently lifting up the hive bodies. He can tell from their weight about how much honey each hive contains. In Minnesota, a colony of bees needs at least a hundred pounds of honey to get through the winter. Those without enough honey have to be fed with sugar syrup.

John's last autumn chore is wrapping the hives. Only beekeepers who live in cold climates provide this winter protection for their bees. John Wetzler wraps his hives in sheets of black plastic and roofing paper. The material will shelter the bees from harsh winds. And its black color will absorb the weak winter sun, helping to warm the hives during the cold months to come.

John wrapping his hives for the winter

Winter snow piled high around John's beehives

The Long, Cold Winter

During December and January, snowstorms bluster through southwestern Minnesota. In this flat prairie region, the wind blows hard, pushing snow ahead of it in squalls and drifts.

In John Wetzler's bee yard, a windbreak of pine trees shelters the wrapped hives. Inside each hive, the bees huddle together in a football-shaped cluster that extends across several frames. As the bees on the outside of the cluster begin to feel the cold, they change places with the bees inside. At the center, the temperature may be as high as a summer-like 90 degrees. Here the queen spends the winter, protected by a living blanket of bees.

As the long days and weeks pass, the bees eat the honey that they have so carefully stored. When the food supply in one part of the hive is gone, the cluster moves to another area where honey is stored. Honey is a high-energy food, and it keeps the bees warm despite the cold.

But on a night when the wind howls and the temperature falls below zero, John Wetzler can't help worrying about his bees. The next morning, the beekeeper puts on his boots and heavy jacket and goes out to the bee yard. He checks to see that the hive coverings are securely fastened.

The beekeeper spends some winter evenings in his basement workshop making new frames for his hives. When the snow melts and warm weather finally comes, the bees will build new cells on these frames. They will fill them to the brim with the first sweet honey of another year.

Melting snow in the bee yard tells the beekeeper that spring is around the corner.

A Note about Commercial Beekeeping

In the United States, there are about 1,600 *commercial beekeepers.* They make up 10 percent of all beekeepers, but they produce around 60 percent of the honey crop. Compared to hobbyists like John Wetzler, commercial beekeepers do everything on a large scale. They own hundreds, even thousands, of hives and often raise their own queens. They also have more elaborate equipment than most hobbyists. In their extracting plants, commercial beekeepers use automatic machines that uncap frames and bottle honey.

In addition to producing honey, some commercial beekeepers rent out their bees to pollinate crops. Many food plants need bees or other insects to carry pollen from flower to flower. This transfer makes it possible for fruits, vegetables, and nuts to develop. Foods such as apples, peaches, pears, cucumbers, melons, blueberries, cranberries, and almonds are all pollinated by bees.

Growers who want to make sure that their crops are pollinated rent hives from commercial beekeepers. The hives are brought to the fields when the plants are in flower and left so the bees can do their work. Some beekeepers use trucks to move their hives all over the country. They may go to Florida when the citrus trees are in flower and then to Maine for the blueberry season. Providing pollination services is a big part of commercial beekeeping.

Today many commercial beekeepers as well as hobbyists are worried about something that may threaten beekeeping in the United States. This is the invasion of Africanized bees. African bees were first brought to Brazil in 1957. They were good honey producers. They were also very defensive, vigorously stinging any intruder that disturbed their hives.

Since the 1950s, descendants of the African bees have been moving slowly northward. In 1990, the first Africanized bees crossed into the U.S. from Mexico. By the end of 1992, the bees had reached the area of Austin, Texas. Experts are not sure how far north they may go. Since the bees originally came from tropical Africa, they may not be able to survive in areas with cold winters.

If Africanized bees do spread, some beekeepers think that they will cause very serious problems. But others believe that the future is not so bleak. In Latin America, beekeepers have learned to live with Africanized bees. U.S. beekeepers are clever and creative people whose business depends on working with bees. They will also find ways of dealing with these aggressive newcomers.

Beekeeping Terms

bee glue: a sticky material that bees make from plant resin and use to seal openings in the hive (p. 7).

brood: eggs and developing young bees (p. 8).

colony: a group of bees made up of one queen, many workers, and a few drones. Each hive contains one colony (p. 5).

commercial beekeeper: a beekeeper who has at least three hundred hives and who makes a living from keeping bees (p. 30).

decapping tank: a tank used to catch wax caps cut from a frame of honey (p. 22).

drone: a male bee (p. 5).

forager: a worker bee who leaves the hive to collect nectar and pollen (p. 14).

foundation: a sheet of wax impressed on both sides with a pattern of honeybee cells. Using the pattern as a base, bees build the wax cells of their combs (p. 4).

frame: the wooden structure that holds foundation (p. 4).

fume board: a board with a cloth pad on which bee repellant is sprinkled (p. 20).

hive body: the wooden box where honeybees live and raise their young (p. 4).

hive tool: a small metal tool used to pry open hives (p. 7).

hobbyist: a beekeeper who keeps bees for a hobby and has no more than twenty-five hives (p. 3).

honey extractor: a machine used to take honey out of the cells of a frame (p. 22).

nectar: a sweet liquid produced by flowers to attract bees and other insects (p. 4).

nectar flow: the kind of nectar being collected in an area at any one time (p. 15).

pollen: a powdery substance in flowers that contains male reproductive cells. When bees visit flowers, they pick up pollen and transfer it to other flowers (p. 14).

queen bee: a female bee able to produce young. Each hive has only one queen (p. 5).

queen cell: the special large cell in which a queen bee is raised (p. 16).

queen excluder: a sheet of plastic with holes in it, used to prevent a queen from getting into a honey super (p. 18).

queenright hive: a hive with a healthy queen who is laying eggs (p. 11).

royal jelly: a food produced by worker bees' bodies that turns a developing bee into a queen (p. 16).

smoker: a device that produces smoke from materials burned inside it. Beekeepers use smoke on bees to quiet them (p. 6).

super: a small box with frames and foundation in which bees store honey. Supers are put on top of the hive bodies (p. 18).

swarming: the division of a hive that takes place when the queen and some of the bees leave to find another home (p. 16).

worker bee: a female bee that does the work of a bee colony. Worker bees normally do not lay eggs (p. 5).

Favorite Honey Recipes

Honey/Peanut Butter Spread

1/4 cup honey
1/4 cup butter or margarine
1/4 cup peanut butter

Mix the ingredients together well, and spread on bread, toast, or English muffins.

Honey/Chocolate Chip/Coconut Cookies

1 1/2 cups flour
1 teaspoon baking powder
1/4 teaspoon salt
1/2 cup shortening or margarine
1/2 cup honey
1 egg
1 teaspoon vanilla extract
1/2 cup chopped nuts
1/2 cup shredded coconut (optional)
1 cup (6 oz.) semisweet chocolate pieces

Preheat the oven to 375°F. Grease 2 cookie sheets.

In a small bowl, sift together the flour, baking powder, and salt. In a large bowl, cream the shortening or margarine and the honey. Beat in the egg. Add the vanilla and the sifted dry ingredients. Fold in the nuts, coconut, and chocolate pieces. Drop from a teaspoon onto the prepared cookie sheets. Bake for 10 to 12 minutes. Makes 2 to 3 dozen cookies, depending on size.

Cocoa with Honey

1 1/2 cups milk
1/4 teaspoon cinnamon, allspice, or cloves
2 tablespoons honey
1 tablespoon unsweetened cocoa powder

Heat the milk until almost boiling. Remove from heat and stir in the cinnamon, allspice, or cloves. Add the honey and cocoa, and beat with a wire whisk until well blended. Makes 1 serving.

"I just like to know," said Pooh humbly. "So as I can say to myself: 'I've got fourteen pots of honey left.' Or fifteen, as the case may be. It's sort of comforting."

—Winnie-the-Pooh
From *The House at Pooh Corner*,
by A. A. Milne